THUG POETRY

Volume 1

ALAN HINES

 www.trafford.com

North America & international
toll-free: 1 888 232 4444 (USA & Canada)
fax: 812 355 4082

Book of poetry already published by Alan Hines,

1. Reflections of Love

Urban Novel already published by Alan Hines,

1. Book Writer

Upcoming books of poetry by Alan Hines,

1. Reflections of Love (Volume 2,and 3)

2. This is Love (Volume 1, 2, and 3)

3. Founded Love (Volume 1,2, and 3)

4. True Love (Volume 1,2,and 3)

5. Thug Poetry (Endless Volumes)

6. When Thugs Cry (Volume 1,2,and 3)

7. A Inner Soul That Cried (Volume 1,2,and 3)

8. Visionary (Endless Volumes)

9. In My Eyes To See (Volume 1,2, and 3)

10. A Seed That Grew (Volume 1,2,and, 3)

11. The Words I Spoke (Volume 1,2 and 3)

12. Scriptures (Volume 1,2, and 3)

13. Revelations (volume 1,2, and 3)

14. Destiny (Volume 1,2, and 3)

15. Trials and Tribulations (Volume 1,2, and 3)

16. IMMORTALITY (Volume 1,2, and 3)

17. My Low Spoken Words (Volume 1,2, and 3)

18. Beauty Within (Volume 1,2, and 3)

19. Red Ink of Blood (Volume 1,2, and 3)

20. Destiny of Light (Jean Hines) (Volume 1,2, and 3)

Upcoming non-fiction books by Alan Hines,

1. Time Versus Life

2. Timeless Jewels

Upcoming Urban Novels by Alan Hines,

1. Queens of Queens

2. Black Kings

3. Playerlistic

4. The Police

5. Scandalous

6. The West Side Rapist

7. Shattered Dreams

8. She Wrote Murder

9. Black Fonz

10. A Slow Form of Suicide

11. No-Love

12. War Stories

13. Storm

14. Ghetto Heros

15. Boss Pimps

16. Adolescents

17. In The Hearts of Men

Acknowledgements

Special thanks to the creator of the Heavens, and the Earth for blessing me with life to live. I thank the creator for putting on heart and mind to become a writer,and I love it; as always I thank the creator for all his many blessings. Special thanks to my grandmother Jean Hines, she's in Heaven; I love you and miss you so much; I'm forever grateful for all love, support, and knowledge you gave me when you was here on earth; I wish you can see me know all the knowledge that you fed me was like nutrion that helped me to grow later in life, and I've really did alot of growing up. Special thanks to my mom, and dad without them from God I wouldn't even exist. Special thanks to my sister Alicia for introducing me to writing books, and being there in my past times of need. Special thanks to Julie Hull (attorney), John Fitzgerald Lyke (attorney), and to Mr. Marasa (English Teacher). And to anybody else that showed me any love, and support throughout life.

Thanks to the entire Hines, and Laughlin family, all my co-workers that's cool, and always asking when the next book coming out not actually interested in reading it, but more interested in my success, that's what I call love. Ricardo Sanchez, for being there in a time when I needed you most. Roscell Hines(Cel), Alan White(Block), Shamon Miller(Pac), I know each one of you got it rough, everyday I pray crying out to the Heavenly Father hoping he see it fit to reverse circumstances. I hope my prayers will be answered.

I've been writing poetry for many years now, and I've wrote alot of books of poetry

that's to be premiered soon. But this is thus far one of my favorite books of poetry

I ever wrote.

Many of my poems in this book revolve around people in prison, and people with immigration problems. I'm not in prison, nor do I have any problems with immigration, thank God; but to a certain extent I can feel they pain.

To all that decides to read it I hope everyone enjoys it.

1. BoardWalk

Down by the Boardwalk wars were fought.

Literature was taught.

Trumpets sounded off, gun fire sought, as blasphemy flowed fluently from mouths.

Shorties was sent off. Lives was lost.

Traps were set, rats, and snakes was caught.

As more guns was brought.

Stool penguins were put out;

Hit in their mouth and hung like the past centuries down south.

Those that won earn respect, and clout, and this came about on California, and Flournoy a place called the Boardwalk.

2. Mexican and black

I can feel your pain.

We're like one in the same.

I cried endless tears when I heard that Immigration came and took you back to Mexico's poverty range.

In Spanish speaking I'd scream blasphemy incentitys of Immigrations name in vain.

If this is a free country why they won't let you remain.

The land of liberty is all a game for personal gain.

I just hate hearing immigrations name, it feels worser than a sickening pain.

I imagine how you felt a mental torture of firely flames, for my ancestors it was the same as slave ships came, being shackled, and chained, stripped of names, whipped with whips inhumanly, like a wild animal being tamed.

Chased down like futuristic centuries war games.

In the blink of an eye circumstances change, amongst cruel, and usual conditions that's derange.

I can definitely feel your pain, because we're one in the same.

3. Blind

E yes closed, as if I'm blind;
blind, going back and forth during this present time.

As fiends constantly in lines, rocks and blows they buying, as drug dealers money inclines.

Lost in a false state of mind.

In the life of mines I caught my fiancee cheating on Valentines with another woman, a female friend of mines, it wasn't her first or last time.

Formulated men of flesh I am.

Living to dying.

Funeral after funeral tears won't even come out to much crying.

Seeing the downfall of those childhood friends, family members, and of mankind.

Sometimes I wish I couldn't see the chaos of wordly crimes, sometimes I wish I was blind.

4. Urgent Message

S he had a urgent message which was practice safe sexing.
Partners get free H.I.V. tested.

Was a mental doctor for kids that had been molested.

Wore only pink to support breast cancer awareness.

Practice non-smoking so she wouldn't catch cancer.

She brought forth urgent messages all along she was already A.I.D.S. infected,

Wanted others to learn from her mistake as lessons.

Until death she spit urgent messages.

5. Beginning

I n the beginning there were Adam & Eve;
a bitten fruit brought forth sin, a deceive, Lucifer achieved,
now comes forth lusting and greed.

Broke and starven, the rich wont feed.

And then came the ViceLords, the Breeds, and the G.D.'s Creeds.
Devilish deeds.

Feds cutting heads bodies fall no one to lead.

Trapped in time frames places don't want to leave.

Getting high as a way to be free.

No since of direction, confused as can be.

Stuck in the dark without a light to see, from the beginning to
infinite.

6. Twins I Never Wanted You To See

Twins I never wanted you to see the shaded side where it's dark.

A teenage mom, once a month waiting on food stamps in the form of a Link Card.

Baby daddy vanish, ventured off somewhere in Mars.

Never wanted you to see hypes with lighters that spark selling their bodies for sums that aren't large.

That's why I preach to you reach for the stars.

Know that it's life beyond the drug dealers with fancy cars.

To me both of the twins are superstars.

I love from near or far.

Earth angels is what you are.

That's why I continuously preach to you about being in the likeness of God.

7. Split Decision

With precision he made a split second decision.

Within gunfire took away a man's existence.

Now it'll be little kids that'll grow up without their father at Christmas.

A mom that will blame herself for her sons life being diminished.

Using the devils inventions, with ill intuitions as his partner told him no he didn't listen.

In a bad split decision he caught a murder with a co-defendant.

Blew trial, natural life was his sentence.

Split decisions.

8. Unproperly Place

A place where grown men cry.

Some hung themselves they'd rather die.

Trapped in cells with Lucifer by their sides.

Overtime family and friends left them behind.

No money orders, no waiting in commissary lines, must grind.

Eyes wide open to the past of being blind, to falsehood of love from mankind.

Unproperly place doing hard times.

9. Progress

Great dreams of projects, prospects.
Disapprovals, protest.
Kept going after rejects, continuous progress.
Cold world didn't get the best.
Not too much stress, exercised was no sweat.
Loved the kids to death.
Would definitely strive for excellence until the last breath.
Life was a test that was passed through progress.

10. Ms. Season

In the Summer she'd shine like the sunlight so bright.

In the Spring is when she'd allow the wonderful joys of life to be seen.

In the fall is when she'd encourage people to stand tall through it all.

In the winter is when she'd be in the holiday spirit, spreading her wealth feeling a privilege in giving.

11. Cold World

Even in the summertime cold minds plot on a new day and age massacre of St. Valetines.

Financial assistance hard to find.

Living to dying, death shall come in due time.

Watch you front and behind.

Criminal minds, even those that make laws commit white collar crimes.

Draw off symbols and signs.

Twins listen to dad as he tell you the truth without lying.

Love all, trust none of any kind, in this cold world the devil design.

12. Repressed

Repressed dreams wanted to live them out like a king.
Until reality came flowing like the Mississippi river of disastrous streams.

Poetry and non-fiction stories being told from the eyes of a dope fiend.

Alienated human beings, poison contaminated queens, premeditated schemes.

Fatherless, troubled teens.

The epidemic of A.I.D.S, poverty, and shattered dreams was waking up, and seen.

Replenished unfinished repressed dreams.

13. A Streets Curse

For you my brother our love never begin at birth.

For I showed love and you used me for what I was worth.

For there was no Holy Divine day, no real praises to the ones that really uplifted that got slayed;

instead you misused me to sell packs, and run your joint so you could get paid.....lead me astray.

For they didn't really abide by the Fataha, the five points of the golden star, the most gracious and merciful one Allah.

The Oath was wrote as only one piece that controlled, shaped and mold, put over eyes a blind fold of those that were in charge that possessed hearts that was so cold.

Till this day a lot of brothers still on count and won't let go.

14. Reality Formed

Once upon a time in America there were artwork, poetic love poems.

Little girls getting their dreams to have pony's and unicorns.

Until reality came in the form of a storm.

Barking dogs sirens and the sounds of burglar alarms.

Killed their own parents, children of the corn.

Behold of the pale white horse with a horn like a unicorn.

Hurricanes, floods, and thunderstorms.

Blood dripping, and pouring.

Continuous deaths, and mourning.

Tormented racist legislative candidates in closets performing.

The last days of revelation is up and forming.....

Reality in its rawest form.

15. No Social

No social, but yet and still I stay close to.

I know what you go through.

Through my pen I write poetry and nonfiction wishing it could actually be true, as citizenship forever comes through.

I'm always praying for each one of you.

Although you speak no English which is a foreign language to you, with all respect due let you have socials, and be considered Americans to.....

16. Growed Up

I growed up in the days of old, silently staring in the mirror reminiscing of my youth turned cold.

By dope fiends, pipe smokers it's was stole, and sold for the low.

Visions of me looking out of project windows and seeing mom, and dad when they were young before substances took control.

Visions of my own kids leading themselves astray, away from the prism of what the creator unfold.

Lucifer's powerful hold control lost souls, those seeking fortune and fame, and the glitter, and gold.

Since the days of old I grew up, I growed.

17. No Love For This Side

Some say it's no love for the other side, in reality it's no love for this side. Brother's kill own

Brother's to die. At the funeral momma cries, but she still continue to get high.

This side will look you straight in the eye and tell a bald face lie.

Shoe laces never learned how to tie.

Father was never by my side, to busy getting high.

Taught my own self how to drive down this bumpy road of being alive.

It aint no love for this side.

18. Thief

S he came to me like a thief in the night.
My heart she stole, I sold my soul.

Her tactics were old, but new to me.

Although I'm from the city's streets, had been around numerous ladies, but she was, she really was something new to me.

She tricked me into being the man she wanted me to be.

Engaged to soon be married.

I love so much that our love affair was horrifying and scary.

Home alone I'd be Tom, she'd be Jerry.

This lady was like Christmas, very merry.

Come to find out she'd been with Tom, Dick, Harry, and even Larry.

Although living she made us all feel legendary!

19. She Had Game

She had more game than Milton Bradley.

Humanized Monopoly, schemed for money.

Each time a man landed on her property they'd have to pay heavily.

Those that was wealthy now lived in poverty;

She tricked them outta all they money.

She talked preacher's into being sinners.

She turned losers into winners.

Those that had finished were back at the beginning.

Her game came from all the things she'd seen.

She even turned filthy animals clean.

She was worst than a drug as men fiend.

Cold as ice the reality from a dream.

She made many men feel like kings.

For her venom was more poisoning than anything ever heard of or seen.

She really did her thing..... she had game.

20. Mexican or Puerto Rican

D idn't know if she was a Mexican or Puerto Rican.
She didn't speak any English.

But her body I was thrill seeking.

Late night creeping.

Away from others I wanted to be fleeing, around her is where I wanted to be in.

She was a beautiful human being;

Smooth creamy skin.

From her stride you could tell she had dignity and pride within.

Friendliness with no end.

Catholic life without sin.

I longed for her nights and days within.

Each time I'd tried to talk she'd say no comprende.

Didn't speak any English.

I wonder is she Mexican or Puerto Rican.

21. Advance

You see how they plotted on you in advance.
Wanted to disarm your successful circumstance.
Get within your wife's pants.
Overthrow you make you feel less than a man.
Wanted your life to come to an end.
Break bread with, hug, and show love, those you call
friends, plotted on you in advance, who knows what's
in the heart of men.....
Plots in advance.

22. Even Though

Even though I loved her so she had devilish tendencies
Like an embryo, anxious to grow.

More concerned with the way my cash flowed, fast instead of slow.

Some considered her a pro.

But as for me I loved her so.

In the cold of below zero I'd walk barefoot in the snow to her place down below.

Even though I loved her so other men have told that behind doors that's closed she was good to go.

Even though she's a pro I still love her so.

23. To Life

S he brought things to life that brought the men out at night.
To life she'd show men just how tight.
Over her the guys would fight.
In her sight she'd see men lining up with money each
night to bring things to life......

24. Life and Death

G od giveth life and only he should have the power to cause death.

    As it shall be no penalties of death by the governor's estate.

No hoodlums shall create casualties of street wars in

lives they can't take.

Fatality must rely through natural causes of faith.....

God giveth life and only he should have the power to take it away.

25. Paradox

A paradox of raging bills that spit.
On pull pits preacher sit scheming on ways to get rich.
Sick sexual cravings that's obviously evident.

Those that prey on those without street sense, common sense, tricking off money spent, young ladies that turn out to do whatever they are sent.

A paradox of nasty dirty old man looking for flesh of teenage kids.

Watching for the police as crimes they commit.

Throwing bricks at the pen begging for a way in.

Curse kids cause of lives of bastard parents sin.

Many men shall burn within the heart of devils firely skin.

This is the life we shall never change, never give in.

Murdering childhood friends, lil grammer school girls pregnant with twins by grown men.

A positive test of H.I.V. as your life shall end.

"This is your brain on drugs," as real brain cells are frying.

Witnessing testifying, grown men crying, the jail cells they shall die in.

Starvation and mayhem.

Puddles of blood new borns lie, and die in, continuous crying.

Ladies bodies perverts buying, in this paradox of eternal life I shall live and my soul shall never die in.....

A paradox of continuous crying.

26. Out of Order

A body of contaminated water.
Missing my daughters.
Affiliated headquaters.
Drugs imported, that customers ordered.
Plans unafforded.
Kids aborted.
Legislative men were extorted.
No law and order.
Immigrants deported;
but Mexicans steady crossing the border,
out of order through the dessert thirsty for holy water.....
Out of order.

27. Blazed

Blazed it with fire, tooking hire.

Stimulational desire.

Clientele grew, as workers continued getting hired.

"Who working, who got that loud fire."

In line mass amount of cash crop buyers, wanting to blaze to be taking higher.

At a young age they felt like they had retired.

Women and men would blaze and stick out their chest

as if they'd conquered a quest.

It was their choice for the best, loved it to death,

blazed it until it was no more left.

28. Said and Done

It was said that she'd love me breathing or dead.
Choice me first before any other men instead.
She did whatever I wanted in the bed.
Eased my mind, relieve stress from my head.
She even spent time with my mom when she was sick in bed.
Had been together through years that past.
One cold day reality had came to drag, code red, code
red as she left me as soon as I got snatched by the feds.
Jumped ship, left town with my money filled in bags.
Done the opposite of what was said.

29. Romance

Around the house topless she'd prance and sometimes tap dance as we'd romance.

At times she'd get on her knees and say I think I can, I think I can, I think I can.

To her I was the world's greatest man;

A God of the ancient Africans as we'd romance.

I was the perfect gentlemen; a lover and a friend.

We'd hold hands and I'd show her off around the men;

No egotistical stuff building within.

I treated her better than any men did or can.

We shall be together to the bitter end, capotilizing

On a romantic and erotic blend.....

A romance that will never shorten, as the completion

Will never begin or even give in.....

Romancing to the end.....

30. Publicize

H ighly publicized.
A musicianist that played the saxophone in jazz.

Within comparison and contrast had more than a little class.

With a body that made me fantasize.

I'd see her on stage, in magazines, in newspapers next to ads.

She was a blast from the past.

Even in the future she'd last.

Famously she was publicized for the attributes she had.

She wrote down expectations, in a pad.

Then brought them to reality publicly as she publicized.

31. 9 Lives

C aught up in the streets 9 lives:
Criminalized, devilish disguise, institutionalize,

Scandalize, utilize, foolish pride, petrified, homicide, dramatized, by living not a double but nine lives, yes, 9 lives.

Criminalized by all the things I did to obtain cash.

Devilish disguise in which no one will never know of my secret nine lives.

Institutionalize, stuck in a mental state of being in hell burning in fire, but still alive.

Scandalize for all the scandalous tricks I did to survive.

Utilize my hands to sharpen knives to use to take away lives.

Foolish pride, not letting things slide wanting to be the emperor of everyone dead and alive.

Petrified others seeing the way I'd ride with a bunch of name brand killers on my side, as inner sickness,

and egotistical dominance collide.

Homicide for those I'd killed not giving them a chance to naturally die.

Dramatized by my own actions of my 9 lives, now I'm ready to die, and put and end to my sickening 9 lives.

32. Living It Up

Why should I live my life in vain,
    when I can be doing all sorts of wonderful things.
    Manuscripts for money exchanged.
Partying with no change.
Celebrating the things that's to come, and have came.
Let freedom ring.
Doing what some dreamed.
Happiness to bring.
Living life like a king.

33. Loving At Its Best

L oving the way you finesse.
Your tender caress.
Love making at its best.
Better than the rest.
Conquered the quest made it a love fest.
No regrets, glad I met, the one I love better than the rest.
Loving at its best.

34. She Wanted To Do It Again

The only female, her, in a room with four men,
As we treated her with no respect as we begin and end.
Videotaped and showed to friends.....
She still wanted to do it again.
For what she did others wanted dividends and to be
Pleasured in the same extent.
She received no dividends and only our pleasure was
Given, but yet and still she wanted to do it again, and again.
In a strange way she felt grand being seduced by more
Than one man, some didn't even know her name was Jan.

As we dropped her off at home it was as she lived in the Hamptons.
Mom and dad had so much money that their back account
Was numberless.
Brought up properly which was evident.
But, some way, somehow she loved committing sins with more than
one man.

Each time the men would dive in unprotecting,

Afterwards she wanted to do it again, and again.

We never could understand why this classy chick Jan

Wanted to do it as we begin less known talking about doing it again.

35. Jewels

Given jewels, a planted seed for harvesting growth that shall someday feed.

Teach and lead.

Give lessons, take heed.

Aim to please.

Drive to succeed.

Study, and read.

Plant seeds that shall grow through eternity.

36. A New Beginning

A life without ending.
A new beginning.
Replenished land of past decisions.

Swerving from crash collisions.

Exiles of tension.

Outdate, no remainder of sentence.

Plushed palace of living existence.

A divine intervention.

A past future of repass existence.

A new.....A new beginning.

37. Ridiculous

She was ridiculous.
Far from a saint like Nicholas.
She was more like the Grinch whom stole Christmas.
The devils misses.
To hostile even for prison.
When she wasn't around I'd miss her.
She was ridiculous but she always let me get it,
and it felt splendid.

38. Motherly Love {Jean Hines}

T hanks for always showing me love.

You always provide clean water as purity from above.

But I was filled with dirt that turned your clean water into mud.

It was as if God cast you from Heaven above.

I was like the Devil's socket as he plugged.

You felt it was better to give than receive.

As for me I done robbed everyone in the country.

You prayed that criminals wouldn't commit crimes

And prisoners would be set free.

I committed so many crimes that I even caught cases

For shooting at the police.

Although I did bad things and ran the streets you always loved unconditionally.

I never directly did anything bad to my motherly.

But my lifestyle made you not able to eat or sleep,

you was never stress free.

I wish I could raise you from the cemetary A.S.A.P.

to return the love and to make you be proud of me.

Motherly love, repeat.

39. Strolls

L et me take you on a stroll where young will turn old.

Food stamps will be like gold.

As you'll come in contact with those you once knew and still know.

Childhood friends continue to grow.

No pressure to fold.

All yeses with no no's.

Peaceful as enemies travel through warzones that's

Old in which they once couldn't go.....

Let me take you on a pleasant stroll.

40. Seek and Find

I n the bible it states seek, and you shall find.
I'm seeking within due time, but it's if the blind
Leading the blind, people steady dying, at funerals
Crying, as some use drugs to ease minds.
Going through hard times.
Some move forth as others remain behind.
Simple minimum wage job, standing in a time line,
Hard to find.
In court those themselves that commit crimes in
Court testifying, and murders continuously incline.
Rocky mountains being climbed, by those that was high
While trying.
Being deaf, blind, retardation in minds, seek and
Find someday a light will shine.
In this life of mines I seek a peace in mind to find
While living instead of when dead from dying.
Seek and you shall find.

41. Dominated

She dominated my existence.
Each time she'd talk I'd vividly listen.
Reminiscing, and kissing.
She was my mistress.
I really wanted her as my misses.
Constant visions of her nudity with precisions.
We'd skinny dip with fishes.
Sneak around others visions.
She had my heart locked away like prison.
She dominated me from near, and a distance.....
My dominate mistress.

42. My Seed

She reminds me of myself when I was once her age.

So young full of life, joyful plays.

An adolescent not imagining the flip side of the page, young ones having sex a few times after virginity being contaminated with A.I.D.S.

Little kids that was murdered by the bullets of strays in playgrounds they once played.

Now in the graves the young ones lay.

Confidential informants having things their way,

As the feds clap and celebrate.

Stool penguins always with something to say.

Brutal beatings by the police officers in rage,

Caught on tape, and still get away.

Yes racism exist to this very day.

In minds descendants of slaves still mentally enslaved.

Lovers faking romance as to capitolize from money

Companions once made.

It is what it is on the back and the front of each

Written page.

My seed is so young can't even see certain things in

The light of days.

I remember when I was once her age now I'm a grown

Man ripped open through my adolescent stage.

43. Secretly

For me she wanted to bleed.
To her I'd won the presidency, and her secret services were in need.

The first time on her knees she wanted it to be with me.

On her back in agony she wanted to plead.

She wanted me to always have loving memories.

Secretly she even wanted me to replace her husband to be.

She wanted to splurge on me expensively.

All the things to be was because she really wanted me.

I never knew none of these things to be, that's

Because she kept them secretly.

44. UnGodly Place

Where memories are erased.
      Companions left now your replaced.
      Dogs and acid in the form of mase.

Smoking cigarettes laced.

Friends defaced, snakes.

An everyday bitter taste.

Smells of toxic waste.

Some with no outdates;

Stuck until another world the creator creates.

Face to face with the judge and state.

No money orders awaiting on the pay by the state.

Family and friends show how fake.

Those praising the devil, middle finger to the pearly gates.

Looking in the mirrors watching a snake.

Right at the end of the sentence catch another case.

This ungodly system of a place.....

45. Judy

She possessed a one of a kind genuine beauty, a cutie.

George Jetson descendants Judy.

A grown up Cliff Hucstable daughter, Rudy.

She had a fact in life like Todie.

Her vocal cord played my instrument as if it was her duty, Judy.

46. Midlife

S he was going through a midlife crisis.
Her teenage son was serving natural life.
Her 14 year old daughter had been pregnant not
Once but twice, until the abortion clinic took
away the unborn life.
She blame it on their dad for not raising them right.
But it was her allowing the kids to grow up seeing
In plain view of visual sight their mom partying
Day and night, bringing different men and women
To her bedroom as genitals collide into sexual fights.
Tight eyes staying high as a kite.
A honest job or college wasn't what she like,
She like to run the streets day and night;
Living on the edge of life.
Her kids became a product of their mother's sinful
Delight, and grew up fast, led astray, wasn't able
To see the truth of prosperous lights,
That shined bright.....crisis of life.

47. Addicted Lands

An castration to men, in the land of quick sands.
Pick pockets work with hands as a bomb on controlled
Substances is supplied because of demand.
I think I can, I think I can be more than a man.
Stuck in powdery sands, trying to get free but can't
When in reality I can.
Tried almost everything against it known to men.
Stopped for a little while but back in lines shopping
Again.....Addicted Lands.

48. Witnessed

She was a Jehovah that bared witness that life
Was for the fulfillment of giving.

Promising and worth living without suicidal intentions.

Eternal life without any finish.

Replenished cleansed sins forgiving.

Parish away false scriptures that was endless.

As infants grow to see a late old age of existence;

Throughout lives making holy decisions.

She'd bare witness that life was for the giving.

49. Determining Factors

Determining factors, disasters.
New born babies being born bastards.
Close caskets.
Improperly disposed of cremated ashes.
Constant cold sweats and troubled flashes of killers
Unmasked, being arrested by force of task,
Living a short life that didn't last.
Family members and friends constantly past.
Happy days turned sad.
Dad's doing time in the feds.
Mom refuse to stop drinking as her liver is at it's
Worst turn bad.
Decisional factors determines happiness turned sad.

50. Enslaved

E nslaved living life walking through a maze.
Being challenged by a different phase each day.
Sleeping in caves.

Living horror stories page by page.

Addicted to control substances in the worsest way.

Walking through sites filled with graves.....

Enslaved, by the things the devil made.....

Enslaved.

51. Red

Her name was Red.
Her name came from all the men blood that had shed.
Being involved with Red, you'd end up dead.

She wouldn't kill you, but her jealous ex-lovers would instead.

A natural red head.

Didn't wear blue or black but red instead.

Black eye line with lip stick of red.

Hand and toe nails she had was always polished red.

She was being investigated by the feds for the controlling substances she had between her legs.

She never knew her mom and dad.

But she'd heard they'd always wear Red.

52. The Bad Side

F ire up one and let me drive.
   As we smoke and ride, try to visualize a bad
      Side where locomotives collide, allies instead of enemies die.

Hideous homicide.

Lil kids smoking crack just to get high, just to get by.

This is your brain on drugs as the egg fries.

All alone in the cold with no one by your side.

Gang banging and waring with no peace treaties to be signed.....

Next time you complain about issues in line,

Let me drive as we smoke and ride, as I'll take

You on a tour of the bad side.

53. Dictionary

She wanted to read my dictionary.

Wanted me erotically realistically instead of imaginary.

She wanted for me to get her pregnant as our kids

Would become hereditary.

I made her feel like a kid, as I was like Santa Claus

Mixed with the tooth fairy.

She wore long dresses like females from Little House On The Prairie.

Underneath was no panties.

I fixed her as if I was a tool man that was handy.

She was sweeter than cotton candy.

She'd listen and studied each word in my dictionary.

54. Wanda

Exercised like Jan Fonda.
The things we did together would eventually make
Her a momma.

Wanda stood on accusations and her promises.

Wasn't like the other women whom caused drama.

Wanda had a heart like a grand momma.

Traveled to Africa and Haiti to embrace her fellow brothers.

Disease free but preached about safe sex to others.

Was faithful to me as a friend and a lover.

As time repeats itself to go further, as for Wanda it

Won't be another.

55. Lost Girl

She was booted and misdirected.
Parents rejecting.
A Christmas tree with no presents.
In the winter time child molesters sweated.
Always had sex with no protection.
Age fourteen with triplets pregnant.
Baby daddy was a peasant; later on she even heard
he use to sleep with faggots.
Made alot of mistakes, to young to learn from lessons.
At sixteen found her body beating to death as a message.
Lost girl the sadness of legends.

56. Brain Storm

Through the brain she created storms through her poems lives were born,

Virgins desired porn, children were that of the corn.

Visualized pale white horses, and unicorns.

Apes, and Gorillas in army uniforms.

She sit back created poetry in an animalistic form.

Even more hardcore than porn.

For nonsense she wasn't going.

Mom was hoing, dad was blowing, moing, and owing.

Her words were showcase worthy of showing.

She lived her life through her poems.

Stayed home alone in her own zone.

Letting memories live on, expressing consent on how

Police brutality and racism was wrong.....

That's why we gave her the name storm.

57. Revolved

He turned around and looked, and paused as he seen a frown on the killers face.

It's as he'd been sprayed in the eye with Roach spray.

Guns upped in his face his money and his life

The men would take, the creator had set a date.

Sealed his fate.

His soul wouldn't never see the pearly gates.

He'd be greeted by the devil holding up a rack.

Enemy of the state.

Burning of the stake for the sins he did revolved his way.

In a casket he lay never been to church or prayed.

The devil has his soul to take.

58. Deceptions

S he'd swallow kids as they count their blessings.
    She'd made preachers, reverends, and deacons
        Come to her for confessions.
She was soothing less stressing.
Seeking thousands nothing less than.
Didn't matter if you was under the six or fin,
Pockets she wanted in.
Even had the thoroughbred players filled with deceptions.
No one took heed to lessons.
But they loved going in her flesh deep within.....
She deceived the men.....deceptions.

59. Jerome Hines

I wanna wake you up from your peaceful dead, give you life instead.

Visualizing the brightness of the smile you had.

Let your kids have a dad.

Your grave site is the saddest of sad.

Endlessly tears will shed.

Jerome live again, eternal life with no end.

60. Name

Her poetry name was Flame.
She'd sat fire to the word play like a game.
Erotically she had men hollering her name.

Her poetry was far from lame.

She was abnormal instead of plain.

I'd stand at attention when the host of the club would say her name, Flame.

She possessed alot of intelligence in her brain.

From her knowledge I could gain.

She was the realist that talked the best game.

She was raw within the poetry she'd slang.

Her poetry even enhance the size my manhood king.

Her poetry name was Flame.

61. Could've, Would've, Should've

What could've, would've, and should've been.

I should've came at you to begin, now I'm wondering

if I will ever see you again, pretty brown skin.

Who knows in the bedroom, you could've made me feel

More than a man.

Could've been my main, pregnant with twins.

Wondering if we could have been.

We could've shared time under the crescent moon of the fin.

I heard she was like me loved to utilize her pen,

Writing poetry and living erotic stories that had no end.

Who knows what ever could've been;

maybe she could've been part of my good and evil twin.

A way to release inner secretive secrets within.

A lover and a friend.

I hope I see you again to see the truth that lies within.

62. Sleepless

S leepless nights.
   Lost of visual sight.
      Venom of snakes that bite.
Wondering what might.
Battling with those that's crucial to fight.
Constant visions of the crucifying of Christ.
Darkness with no light.
Sick sinful delights.
Can't sleep because the loud sounds of gun shots each
night, people screaming rocks and blows park all
night; although I know they trying to get they money
right I still can't sleep at nights.

63. Stole

S piritual verses was stole and sold, left out in the cold.
Young men instantly turned old.
Killers that fold.

False stories being told.

Clowns that mold.

Never getting out on parole.

Not being able to pay what is owed.

Lives were brought, resold, and then stole.

64. Before and After Apartheid

B efore and after Apartheid Ethiopians starving dying.
Not even dodging the agonizing noise of flies.
   Stuck in preferential times.
Years later blacks just found out Coretta Scott
King had died.
The falsehood of living lives in lies.
Black on black crimes.
In graves civil rights activist reside each one
Turning in their graves one at a time for sickening
Never ending black on black crimes,
Criminal ties, Satan's enterprise.

65. Passionate Cries

Most was killed only a few naturally died.
A criminal enterprise of scandals, being scandalize.
Foolish pride.

Saints that lust for sexual desires with juveniles.

The devil took off his mask searching for allies.

He looked to his back and seen the world of people

Following him from behind, all eyes wide open wasn't

In the blind.

Passionate cries of how the devil control minds.

66. God of Life

Despite of my faults, wrongs and rights;
you showed me love through your power, will, and might.

You giveth me sight to see the days of light.

I'm your child you brought me to life.

In my dreams you gave me a bronze pen told me poetry,

And stories I was destine to write, don't worry about

Some that will dislike.

All my life you've been by my side through every step and stride.

For our sins crucified, you sacrifice your only begotten son's life.....

That's why I pray to you through your son's name

Jesus Christ each day and night.....

God of life.

67. Brisk

A brisk walk in the park.
Trouble was soon to start.
A stick up kid that loved to rob.
Caught a couple making love in the dark on a bench
Under the stars.
Immediately upped on them robbing them for everything
Even the keys to their car.
He turned around and swiftly tried to depart as a gun blast blew half his back apart shattering his heart.

A brisk walk in the park turned into death thus far.

68. Christ

There was nothing nice about the crucifying of Christ.
But it is a delight to have Christ in our life.
His spirits shines an inspirational light.
Jesus Christ what a great delight.
Against Satan forever on strike.
As holy scriptures be as a manual guide to my life.
What a wonderful life, Jesus Christ thanks for the
sacrafice.

69. A Man I Am

S earching the word for some understanding.
Statue of liberty no longer standing.
Demanding that appeals are granted.
Trying to escape foreign lands, harsh circumstance.
Finally becoming a man, dodging the dragons slaying.
No new or old friends.
Being who I am.
Letting my shark infested past go for a swim.
A grown man, I am.

70. Problems

When problems occur some people turn to the bottle
to see a better day tomorrow.
Getting by rather it's begging or borrow.
Steady drinking drowning in sorrows.
Carrying a load of cargo.
In unhappy marriages, or relationships never
wanting to let go.
Reducing fat with lypo.
Falsified legal documents claimed as typos.
Not realizing that the Heavenly Father is the
answer to sorrows, the only one that definitely
can have you seeing a brighter day, today, and tomorrow.

71. Grind

An invitational grind.
Little did I know she dreamed of being mines.
Sincerly loved my poetic rhymes.

Complimented, said I was best of my time.

We entertwine, in no time she fell in line.

Kept her mouth close, as we wined and dined.

No drama, ever crossed her mind.

She seen what was going on wasn't in the blind, She knew with others I'd creep off all the time.

But yet and still she respected my grind.

She kept encouraging me to write, stay focus, and grind.

At times I'd make love to her body and mind.

As I stayed on the grind.

72. Fruitfully Live

L
ive and let live.

Expect nothing in return, genuinely give.

Spread love and wealth each day of the year, making it merry like Christmas, and happy like it's always a new year.

Show growth in every prominent direction you steer.

Each morning awake to thank God you're still here.

73. Colors Bring

For the colors that you bring I smile and sing.
You make the best out of any and everything.
A realist no one could sell you a dream.
My princess and my queen, my everything.

The colors you bring gleam more than anything I've
ever seen.

Yellow, pink, purple, orange, red, and green, when
the skies turn black thats when we would do our thing.

The colors that you bring is my everything.

74. R.I.P.

I n loving unforgettable fun memories of the way
things use to be.
Through heavens gates you were freed.
Remembered the good you did for me.
Taught me mentally to emburke up the tallest tree.
To be all I can be, and that the world was for me
to see.
Groomed me to be the way I be.
Showed love unconditionally.
Tatoos and t-shirts of those that's deceased.
Once my sorrows, and pains are eased, and our souls
meet, family, and friends shall definitely remember
me.
Unforgettable, unforgottable, unforgettable,
memories of those that's rest in peace, wishing life
repeats.

75. Episode

E pisode after episode, guns that explode, unload.
Homeless that live off in the cold, froze.
Lost souls in which Satan controls.

By prison childhoods, and youthfulness was stole.

Stool penguins told, in state, and federal penitentiary some will stay until they are real old.

Game that's use to strike gold.

Parents showing kids survival tactics as a way

to mold, to live in this world that's so cold,

like the North Pole.....

Episode after episode.

76. Wise Word Quotes

Through it all never let them see you sweat.

Let loose of constant regrets, start feeling blessed.

Prepare for the worst but hope for the best.

Never settle for less.

Hold your head up and stick out your chest.

Learn lessons from each pass or failed test,

and continue to strive for excellence in oneself.

77. Formulated Plan

A formulated plan, was suppose to become a made man, things didn't go as plan.

Water breaking dams.

Floods because there were no sewer system upon land.

At first he started getting alot of money now stuck

in a jam.

Sirens, and handcuffed hands.

Going to the station getting processed in.

Trying to serve weight got him slammed in the end.

78. Her Love Was Fantastic

K indness and love, she brought it, and bring it,
glorified, and singed it.
    In the bedroom she gave me the crown, crowned me
kings of kings at it.
Loving that was automatic.
Free from drama and static.
A active pro at it.
Her love was fantastic.

79. Head To The Sky

Keep your head to the sky, never let your inner spirit die.

  Don't waste time letting life pass you by.

Give life a try.

Don't use pretend fake reasons why.

Be honest with yourself without living a lie.

We are all living to die so be grateful that you are

still alive.

Without no false reasons why, be proud keep your head to the sky.

80. Should

B reak the chains of monotony.
Playing Charades, and Monoply doing strange things to get money off others people property.

Saying what if, what might, probably.

Walking around feeling sorry.

Arise from sickness and poverty.

Be strengthen in come about triumphantly.

Find pleasant residence that is of heavenly.

Live life with a mental capacity of being wealthy.

81. Could've Been Dead

I just remembered what had happen and what was said.
I'f I chose to take that route that day I could've been dead.
Thank God for condoms or the virus that causes
A.I.D.S. I could've had unknowingly to spread.
Witness blood that shed by knives, and led.
Knowledgeable to not go astray or be misled.
Smart enough to watch my front, not just my back instead.
Still living, thank God I aint dead.

82. A Good Kisser

I'd sit and watch a part of me as she bowed down to her knees perform the best intamacy intimately istantly making orgasm be free.

She did so good that I nicknamed her lovely, because

she did it as if she actually loved me..

In the midst of all the pleasing me she had my mind

and body feeling free.

Mentally I'd be mountain climbing, swinging free tree to tree like the monkeys be.

A grown man I be.

I could see all other things that made me happy,

momentarily stress free.

She was a keeper the way she did me as I hum as I'd

release, let it all out free.

She gave such a great performance as I'd always say

repeat.

83. Planted Knowledge(Jean Hines)

S he said life was for the giving so I gave.
Before crossing the street look both ways.

She said once upon a time men lived in caves,
used sticks to set a firely blaze.

She told me about history in which Africans were
took from the motherland brought to America to be
slaves, even after the 4th of July, Independence
day.

She told me to always honor my mother, and father
in everyway, although God is the reason kids are made.

Follow the word in which the testament conveyed.

Praise his name each day, ignore the Devil never
give him the time of day to lead you a astray.

Let it be done on earth as it is in Heaven tomorrow,
today, and yesterday.

Like a prophet I'd always listen to words you'd say.

You told me that you'd love me even when the

Heavenly Father would take your soul to Heaven to stay.

To this day I still remember the knowlegde and

love you gave.

Although in a grave you lay memories shall never fade, I love you so much in a special way, wish I

could stop crying to whip the tears away.

84. Generations

A generated black plague nation.
Still flagging confederation, after the defeat,
longful frustration.

Minds of enslaved slave trading.

Kidnapping, and slaying, no playing, no hostage

negotiating.

A black plague nation of gang affiliation that's

killing off on races.

Shocked out wacked patients.

Peace officers steady wrongfully killing off the

black nation.

Grand jury stipulated, stated no probable cause

to indict on this past, present, and future date;

in the back of their minds it was a justified

crime of hate for the white supremacy sake, straight snakes.....

Generation of a black plague nation.

85. Dear Heavenly Father

Dear Heavenly Father,

Thank you for giving me life and love regardless.

Pushing me to go futher.

Being a father when my biological didn't bother.

Being a sheild from revolvers.

A problem solver.

A mental doctor.

Most of all thanks for being marvelous.

86. Stimulater

She was a mind stimulater.
A motivater.
A masturbater.
A great debater.
Others would see us together and instantly turn
into jealous haters.

She could stimulate peace into an alligator.
She allowed me to be a baby maker.
An innovator.
An inspirator.

For my needs she'd cater.
I needed no substances because she was my stimulater.

She was the best I ever dated.
A stimulater that recently got her degree and graduated.

87. Singer

She'd sing, sing as she'd wanted freedom to ring.
She'd idolize Dr. Martin Luther as king of all kings.
She designated a place in her home to rehabilitate
drug fiends.
She ate healthy, and kept her body and mind clean.
All alone she'd sing, write music, and poetry,
that was her thing.
She wanted the world to sing, as freedom ring.
The money she made wasn't a thing, to charity
events and those with less than she'd give
up everything.....
A singer that sing.

88. Ridiculous

R idiculous
  Pernicious
  Suspicious
Escape Risk
Fights Fixed
Sliding Risk
Poking St.Nick
Pastors That's Hypocrites.....
Ridiculous

89. Sweetest Hangover

She had the sweetest love hangover.
I never wanted to get over.
Forget ever being sober.
Let her fountain of alcoholic love runneth over.
Staying young never getting older.
A load off my shoulders.
She had the sweetest love hangover.

90. East

F acing the east.
Crushing Satan dragon of the beast.
No Swine to eat.
No homosexuality.
Holy and divinely.
Merciful to thee.
Sun rises in the east.
For I am you, you are me.

91. R.I.P. George Hines(Hubby)

To his funeral most of the family didn't even come.
No tears, to run.
The love was none.
That's why I stay strap with two guns, gasoline,
and a firely wand.
Love all trust none.
When I come across phonies I shall not run,
hold my head to the sky, and my hand on both guns.

On many occasions family, and friends showed me how
phony they was.
But yet and still how could his funeral be empty
as a scorching desert under the sun.

Took me a for a trip of outcomes, no where to run,
and for all one day it was sure to come;
you should love your family by the tons but in reality self
preservation is number one!

92. Jennifer Capricon

J ennifer Capricon loved going horseback riding,
and riding the horns of unicorns.
The queen of porn.
With it in her mouth she'd wish she was born.
Stayed douching kept it clean, and warm.

A replica,
A duplicate,
A hardcore form,
She was down for whatever, she was going.....
Jennifer Capricorn.

93. Tears

As tears ran from his eyes he looked at me and calmly replied, "my appeal was denied."

On death row he'll reside.

Shortly in the electric chair he must fry and

hideously die.

Although they're other appeals in time, but time

wasn't on his side.

He'd read the bible, and exercise to ease his mind.

Sharpen up knives to survive, fist fights with other

inmates from time to time, trouble wasn't hard to find.

No love letters or money orders coming in from the outside.

To the free world it's as he'd already died.

Could'nt sleep crucifying of Jesus Christ haunted

his mind.

I could feel his pain because his problems
wasn't even close to being worser than mines.

Years later the state put him to rest, in the electric chair he was
killed, died in.

I shall shed no tears as men continue dying.

On death row I to reside, so you aint even gotta ask
on who's next in line.....

94. Blemish

A great assistance.
A premonition for me to make wise decisions.
Watched and listen.
Studied pass missions.
Abided by certain policies preached about by Christians.
The future to come would be free from blemish.

95. Global Warnings

She gave global warnings about thunder storms
that were coming.
Illegal drugs flooding the streets in abundance.
Women giving love and in return wanting something.
The mark of the beast was up and running.
The last days was coming.
She always gave global warnings about something
that actually was coming.

96. Stuck In This Game

S tuck in this game searching for fortune as a
drunken pilot flies a plane, lives rearranged.
    Utilizing of control substances to maintain.
Dumb decisions of shame.
Stuck in this game chasing fortune and fame as
rocks people slang for financial gain.

Stuck in this game, some will never change as no friends to claim.
Don't even remember names and it was only momentary
space being exchanged.
Stuck in this game.

97. Role Model

S he was a positive role model.
Didn't drink, but poured liquor out the bottle
for those that wouldn't live to see tomorrow.
Stuggled by herself didn't beg or borrow.
A leader never followed.

Taught people how to live and let go.
On Christmas gave gifts to Santa helped him through
the snow as the gifts was passed out door to door.
With students everything she learned she let them
know.

Some say she was from a foreign land or from another coast, either
way she was a positive role model.

98. Deserve It

One thing is for sure two things are for certain.
I'm ridding myself of a clowns burden.
Royalties I'm earning, I deserve it.
Success dreamed of it, in my sleep heard it.
Worded it, preferred it.
National best sellers list deserve it.

99. A.I.D.S.

R olling dice, she loved losing in strip poker
and Charades.
　　She hung out with Lesbians and gays.
Showed off her nude skin at parades
So you can imagine the image in the bedroom she'd
portray.
Promiscuous sexual partners had it their way.
Lived life sexually, each day was a holiday.
Led herself astray.
H.I.V. test positive for full blown A.I.D.S.
Left the free clinic with nothing to say.
Wanted to change her ways, catch the holy ghost,
and become a part of the lords enchanting array,
not sincerly fake; but it was to late, she'd
soon lie in a grave.
It rained on her parade.
Welcome to the world of A.I.D.S.

100. My Eternal Sleep

I wonder who will be there in my time of despair
to show love, their last respect, that they really care.
Tears and sorrows they'll share.
Will me being in a casket be like a nightmare
of a reality scare, and shall my enemies be happy
that I'm no longer here.
Will I be heavenly or pushed down to the devil's
layers.
Will my seeds turn out to be that of lawyers, doctors, mayors, or
shall they be criminalistic burden bearers.
I wonder who will even show up to the funeral who will even be
there.

Living to dying.
Tears of men.

This is several Chapters of Alan Hines Queen of Queens

QUEEN OF QUEENS
BY
ALAN HINES

Prologue

It was the summer of July 4th 1971, 11:30 P.M.,in Chicago as the fireworks lit up the skies.

Chapter 1

"You sure this the right spot man" Slim asked? "I'm positive this is the right spot, I wouldn't never bring you on no blank mission," Double J said.

With no hesitation Double J kicked in the door and yelled, "Police lay the fuck down".

Double J and Slim stormed in the crib with guns in hand ready to fuck a nigga up if anybody made any false moves.

As they entered the crib they immediately noticed two women sitting at the table; the women was getting ready to shake up some dope.

One of the women laid on the floor face down, crying out "please, please don't shoot me".....

She had seen many t.v. shows and movies in which the police kicked in doors and wrongfully thought an individual was strap or reaching for a gun when they wasn't, as the police hideously shot them taking their life line from em.

The other woman tried to run and jump outta the window; before she could do so Double J tackled her down and handcuffed her.

Double J threw Slim a pair of handcuffs, "handcuff her", Double J said. As Slim begin to handcuff the other chick he begin thinking to himself,were the fuck this nigga get some motherfucking handcuffs from.

The woman that was on the floor crying looked up and noticed that Slim wasn't the police.

"You niggas ain't no motherfucking police,"she said. Double J ran over and kicked her in the face,and busted her nose.

"Bitch shut the fuck up",Double J said.She shut up,laid her head on the floor.As her head was filled with pain,while tears ran down her face,with blood running from her nose she silently prayed that this real life nightmare would come to an end!

Simultaneously Slim and Double J looked at the table filled with dope. Both Slim and Double J mouths drop;they'd never seen so much dope in their lives.Right in front of their eyes was 100 grams of pure uncut heroin.

Both women laid on the floor scared to death;they'd never been so scared in their natural lives.

Double J went into the kitchen found some zip lock bags,came back and put the dope in them,and then stuffed the dope in the sleeves of his jacket cause it was too much dope to fit in his pockets.

"Man we gotta hurry up,you know the neighbors probably heard us kick the door in,"Slim said."The neighbors ain't heard shit cuz of all the fireworks going off.That's why I picked this time to run off in here,while the fireworks going off so nobody won't hear us,"Double J said. "Shiit they could've still heard us,the fireworks ain't going off inside the building,"Slim said."Don't worry about it,"Double J said.

"Lord lets search the rooms before we leave,you know if all this dope is here it gotta be some guns or money in here somewhere,"Double J said."Yep,Jo I bet you it is,"Slim said.

Double J walked over to the woman whom nose he busted kneeled to his knees put a .357 to her ear and clicked the hammer back.

The woman heard the hammer click in her ear,she became so scared that she literally shitted on herself.

"Bitch am a ask you one time,where the rest of that shit at,"Double J asked in a deep hideous voice? She begin crying out and yelling,"it's in the closet in the bottom of the dirty cloths hamper."

Double J went into the closet snatched all the cloths outta the hamper and found ten big bundles of money.He seen a book bag hanging in the closet,grabbed it and loaded the money in it.

Double J went back into the front room, without second guessing it he shot both women in the back of their heads two times a piece.

Double J and Slim fled from the apartment building,got into their steamer and smashed off.

As Double J drove a few blocks away Slim sat in the passenger side of the car looking over at Double J pissed off.

"Lord,why the fuck you shoot them ho's,"Slim asked with hostility? "Look at all the money and dope we got,"Double J said."What that gotta do with it,"Slim asked? "You know that,that wasn't them ho's shit,they was working for some nigga,and if that nigga ever found out we stuck him up for all that shit he'd have a price on our heads.Now that the only people who knew about us taking that shit is dead,"Double J said. Yeah you right about that,Slim thought to himself as he remained silent for a few seconds.....

"You just said something about dope and money,what money,"Slim asked? "Look in the book bag,"Double J said.

Slim unzipped the book bag and it was as he'd seen a million dollars.His mouth dropped,amazed by all the money that was in the book bag.

They hit the e-way and set fire to a lace joint as they begun to think of all of the things they'd be able to do with the money and dope.....

Double J and Slim were two petty hustlers looking for this one big lick,and they finally got it.

They had various hustles that consist of robbing,car theiving,and selling a little dope. All their hustles revovled around King Phill. King Phill was a king of a branch of ViceLords,the(I.V.L.) Insane Vice Lords. They'd rob,steal cars,and sell dope through King Phill,one way or the other.

Double J and Slim were basically King Phill's yes men. Whatever Phill would say or wanted them to do they'd say yes to.

After 45 minutes of driving they parked the steamer on a deserted block where there was no houses,only a big empty park.

Double J begin wiping off the inside of the car.Slim begin to do the same.

"Make sure you wipe off everything real good,we don't wanna leave no fingerprints,"Double J said."You aint gotta tell me, that's the last thing I wanna do is get pinched for a pussy ass stick up murder,"Slim said.

Double J put the book bag on his back and they left the car wiping off the inside and outside door handles and they begin walking to Double J's crib,which was about thirty minutes away.

"Lord fire up one of them lace joints,"Slim said."Here you fire it up,"Double J said as he passed the joint to Slim. Slim instantly set fire to it.They walked swiftly to Double J's crib,continuously puffing on the lace joints.

Once they made it halfway there,out of nowhere,Double J stopped in his tracks.

"What the fuck you stop for,"Slim asked? "Lord we gotta get rid of that car,"Double J said."Why,"Slim asked? "Cuz,like you said we don't wanna get pinched for no stick up murder.If somebody seen that car leave the scene of the crime and they tell the police and the police find the car and dust it for fingerprints,and find one fingerprint that matches one of ours we booked. We'll be sitting on death row saying what we should've,would've,and could've done,"Double J said."How we gone get rid of it,"Slim asked?

"Here take my gun and bookbag,and meet me at my crib,my girl there she'll let you in,"Double J said.

"You still didn't answer my question,"Slim said. "Whats that,"Double J asked? "How we gone get rid of the car,"Slim asked? "Don't worry about it,I got it,"Double J said. "Let's get rid of it together,"Slim said. "Naw man we need to make sure the money and dope is safe,and we need to get these hot ass guns off the streets,"Double J said. "Where is the dope,"Slim asked?

Double J reached in his sleeves pulled out the dope and handed it all to Slim as they departed and went their separate ways.....

I hope this nigga don't get caught fucking around with that car, Slim thought to himself.

Double J went back to the car looking for something to use to set it on fire with.

He ended up finding some charcoal fluid in the trunk of the car,struck a match and threw it on the car as it instantly begin burning.

Double J took off running.He ran halfway home,and walked the other half.

Once Double J made it home,before he could even knock on the door or ring the doorbell Slim opened the door. Double J rushed in nervously and slammed the door behind himself and frantically locked it.

"Nigga what the fuck took you so long,"Slim asked? "What took me so long,shiiit I ran halfway back,but anyway I took care of the business,I burned the car up,"Double J said.

"How much dough we got,"Double J asked? "I don't know I ain't even open the book bag up,I was waiting to you get here,"Slim said. "See thats why I fuck with you,anybody else would've played me for some of the money and dope,"Double J said. "You my nigga I would'nt never try to get over on you.To keep it real, you didn't even have to take me on the lick with you,"Slim said.....

They went into the bathroom,locked the door and begin counting the money.Each bundle of money was a G.

"Damn lord we got 10 stacks and all this dope,"Slim said.

"How we gone get rid of all this dope,"Double J asked? "We gone sell it in grams,"Slim said. "Naw man we need to sell it in bags,we'll make more money selling it in bags.The only problem is where we gone sell it at,you know anywhere we try to open up at they gone close us down,"Double J said. "We gone sell it in the hood,"Slim said. "Stop playing you know damn well we dead in the hood. You know if we open up in the hood they gone close us straight down,"Double J Said. "We gone have to go through Phill,"Slim said. "Yeah we'll get up with Phill tomorrow,"Double J said.

"Man don't tell nobody where we got the dope from,"Double J said. "Nigga,do I look like a lame to you? What the fuck I look like telling somebody about what we did,"Slim said.

"I'm finna go to sleep,you might as well spend a night,"Double J said. "Yeah I might as well spend a night,"Slim said."I'll holla at you in the morning,I'm sleepy as hell,"Double J said as he started to yawn. As Slim went and laid on the couch in the living room. Double J went into his bedroom undressed down to his boxers and t-shirt and got into bed with his wife who he assumed was asleep.

As Double J pulled the covers back he noticed that his wife was in bed asshole naked.

I'm glad I married her,Double J thought to himself while enjoying the view.....

Slim and Double J stayed awoke for a little while thinking about the money they had and the profit they was going to make off the dope.....

As Double J closed his eyes to go to sleep he felt his wife's hands gently slipping into his boxers rubbing on his dick.

"I thought you were asleep,"Double J said."I ain't sleep,I was just laying here thinking about you,"she said.

She continued rubbing on his dick.

"Now you know you can't be rubbing on my dick without any lubrication.That shit don't feel good when you do it with dry hands,"Double J said.

She got up and squeezed a little Jergens in the palm of her hand,as he slipped his boxers off and laid back on the bed.

She grabbed his dick firmly,begin lathering it up with the lotion and jagging him off at the same time.

As she thoroughly jagged him off he pumped her hand until his nut unleashed on her titties,as she begin rubbing the nut around on her titties as if it was baby oil or lotion.

She then took his dick into her mouth gobbling it and the lotion in all swirling her tongue around it and sucking on it as if she was trying to suck some sweet nectar out of it.

Once it got rock hard she begin deep throating it,choking herself with his dick while rubbing on her own clitoris roughly while humming.

In no time flat he was releasing a load of nut down her throat.

She stood up,wiped her mouth and slightly begin growling she then got on top of him and played with his dick for a few seconds until it got back hard.

She looked him in his eyes,as she grabbed his dick firmly and shoved it in her pussy,and begin smiling.....

She begin riding it slowly to get her pussy totally wet,as he grabbed her ass cheeks guiding her movements.

Once her pussy got wet he begin slamming his dick in and out of her,enjoying the tightness of her moist pussy.As she clawed his chest moaning in the midst of pleasure and pain;she liked when it hurted.

It felt so good to him that every time he'd slam his dick up in her pussy it felt like he was actually nutting each time.

As Double J begin to nut,she was cumming simultaneously as he begin to slam his dick in and out her pussy rougher and harder,she begin fucking him back;it was like a rodeo show as their orgasms exploded.

"Get up,get on the bed so I can hit it from the back,"Double J said.She got on all fours on the bed.

Double J got on his knees right behind her and began squeezing and rubbing her big brown pretty ass cheeks.

"Tell me you love me before you start fucking me,"she said."I love your hot ass,"he said.

Double J then rammed his dick in her hot pussy gripping her ass cheeks and slamming his dick in and out her pussy hard and fast while admiring the way her ass cheeks bounced.

In no time he was letting another nut explode in her pussy.

"Let me suck it,"she said in a low seductive tone."Hold on let me roll up a joint,"Double J said."You know that I don't like the smell of lace joints,why you got to lace your weed with cocaine? Why you can't smoke regular weed like everybody else,"she said.

Double J begin smiling,and looking her straight in the eyes.

"We'll I'll smoke a regular joint just for you,"Double J said.

He rolled up a regular joint with only weed in it. Set fire to it as she got on her knees with an aim to please.

As he inhaled and exhaled the potent weed smoke she simultaneously sucked his dick utilizing a suction method sucking mainly the tip thoroughly.

From the potent effect of the weed,combined with her superb suction method, and the moisture of her mouth felt so good that within seconds he released a glob of nut in her face.

He finished smoking his joint and both of them laid on the bed.

"You must really been wanting to fuck?,"Double J asked. "I been thinking about you all day at work. I had to take off work because I creamed in my panties daydreaming about your dick going in and out my pussy and mouth. I been sitting in the house all day waiting on you,"she said.

I done married a freak,Double J thought to himself.

They begin to tell each other how much they loved one another.And how their lives wouldn't be the same without each other,before both of them fell

into a deep sleep.....

The next morning after Double J's wife had went to work Double J and Slim sat at the kitchen table eating breakfast,reminiscing about the stick up and the murders.

They glorified and celebrated the stick up and the murders as if they were professional athletes that just won a championship game,or as if they had won the lottery.

It's sad how bloodshed make others glad.But this life some live as thugs consist of no love.

Other people were brought up to increase the peace and strive to earn college degrees,and live the American dream.

But those that live the street life thrive on death and destruction;they rob,steal,and kill with no discretion,and glorify others name that do the same.....

"Hurry up and finish eating so we can go holla at Phill,"Double J said."I'm already finished,"Slim said. "Well empty the rest of that shit that's on the plate in the garbage and put that plate in the sink,"Double J said.

Slim emptied the rest of the food in the garbage and put the plate in the sink,and went and grabbed the book bag.

"Naw we gone leave the dope and shit here unless you wanna take your half to your house,"Double J said."It's cool,I'll leave it here,"Slim said.

As they rode up the block in the hood where Phill was they noticed many of the Insanes on Phill's security as usual.

Once they made it to where Phill was,Phill began smiling cuz he was happy to see them he needed them to take care of some business for him.

King Phill was a pretty boy.Stood about 6'5 half latino,half black with naturally curly black hair in his mid twenties.

For those that didn't know Phill personally that would've never believed that he was a king of a large street gang.King Phill looked like a pretty boy college student.....

"Park the car I need to holla at ya'll,"Phill said.

They parked and got out to holla at him.

"I need ya'll to get some steamers for me,"Phill said. "We ain't on no car thieving shit right now,we need your assistance on some other shit,"Double J said. "What ya'll need?"Phill asked.

"Let's step away from everybody it's personal,"Slim said.

As they stepped away from everybody else Phill begin trying to figure out what Double J,and Slim wanted. Maybe they finna ask for some shit Phill thought to himself.

"Phill we got some dope we need to get it off,"Double J said. "What you talking about,"Phill asked? "We need to pop it off in the hood,"Slim said. "What ya'll talking about opening up a dope spot in the hood,"Phill asked? "That's exactly what we're talking about,"Slim said. "You know ya'll can't work in the hood if ya'll ain't a 5 star universal elite,"Phill said. "I told him,"Double J said. "Well make us universal elites,"Slim said.

Phill begin laughing.....

"I don't just give out status like that, I ain't one of these phony ass nigga's that let people buy status, you gotta earn it fucking with me," Phill said.

Slim looked at Phill like he was crazy.....

"Earn it, all the shit we do for you, and for the hood. While them niggas you made universal elites be in the Bahamas some motherfucking where, we be doing all the shootings for the hood, and all type of other shit for you and the hood," Slim said. "Yeah you do got a point, cuz ya'll do stand on nation business. This what I'm going to do for ya'll. Am a let ya'll work in the hood under my name, but ya'll gotta pay," Phill said. "How much we gotta pay," Slim asked? "That depends on how much dope ya'll got," Phill said. "We got ten grams," Double J said..... He was lying. "Ten grams that ain't shit. Ya'll work them ten grams for two or three weeks outta Argale park. In two or three weeks ya'll should've atleast double or tripled them ten grams. Once ya'll do ya'll gotta give me a stack every week," Phill said.....

Double J and Slim looked at each other smiling noing it was finna be on.

"A stack a week we got you," Double J said.

"We'll holla at you, I gotta go pick my girl up from work," Double J said..... He was lying.....

As Double J and Slim got into the car and rode off listening to Al Green's Love and Happiness they were happier than a kid on Christmas Day.....

Chapter 2

Three Days Later

"How much is that small black digital scale," Double J asked the cashier? "That one right there is a hundred dollars. But I'd recommend this white one right here if you're going to be weighing things over twenty eight grams. Alot of customers usually buy that small black one, then later on down the line the same customers come back and buy a bigger one, which is a waste of money to me," the woman cashier said. "How much do the white one cost," Slim asked? "Two hundred," the cashier said. "We'll take it," Slim said. "Will that be it," the cashier asked? "Naw we need five bottles of dorms, and a bundle of them little black baggies right there, and two of them mac spoons," Slim said.....

As other customers walked into small record store the cashier paused and begun covering up the small area where contraband was being sold.

"Thomas, can you service the new customers," the female cashier said to her co-worker.....

"Wait til these customers leave, then I'll give ya'll, ya'll items," the female cashier said to Double J and Slim.....

"Ya'll sell scales, baggies, and all type of shit to everybody in the city, and now you wanna act like it's top secret," Slim said. "Yeah we do supply alot of people with contraband, but those are only the people that come in here asking for it. We can't have contraband on display because it's all type of people that come in here. A person might come in here with their kids. Or an off duty police officer might come in here to buy some records. And if they see all of this contraband on display they'll report our ass to the city. We won't loose our store or anything like that, but we'll have to pay a healthy fine," the cashier said.....

Within minutes the other customers purchased their records and left the store.....

"Your total will come out to $375.00," she said.....

Slim paid her and they left the store.....

Once they made it to Double J's crib they immediately weighed the dope for the first time.....

"Damn lord we got a hundred grams, I thought it'll be about fifty grams," Slim said. "Yeah me to," Double J said. "Aw we finna put up numbers if this shit is a bomb," Slim said. "Showl is," Double J said.

"Why did you buy baggies instead of aluminum foil," Double J asked? "Cuz we gone put the dope in the baggies, we don't need no aluminum foil," Slim said. "But we need to put it in the aluminum foil so it can stay fresh," Double J said. "Once we put it in the baggies, then put some thick clear tape on the baggies the dope will stay fresh," Slim said.

"We need to find us a connect on some quinine," Double J said. "Naw we aint gone put no quinine or none of that other crazy shit on the dope. We either gone use dorms or sell it with no mix on it at all," Slim said.

"We gone put three pills on each gram of dope," Slim said.

"How many grams we gone bag up the first time," Double J asked? "We gone bag up ten grams first and put it out there and see what it do, you know we can't bag up to much cuz if it don't sell quick enough it'll fall off," Slim said. "That's my point exactly, that's why I ask," Double J said.

Double J weighed out ten grams on the scale. Then Double J and Slim opened up thirty dorms which was actually capsules. Double J and Slim then grabbed two playing cards a piece and begin mixing the dope with the dorms.....

"How many mac spoons we gone use," Double J asked? "We gone give up two macs for a sawbuck and see how that go first. I'f the dope is a bomb we gone drop down to one mac spoon or a mac and a half. That all depends on how good the dope is. And if it's real good we gone put more dorms on it," Slim said.

Double J and Slim grabbed a mac spoon a piece and begin measuring the dope, and putting it in the bags.....

"I got some thick clear tape in my room in the closet," Double J said. "Wait to we get finished before you go get it," Slim said.....

After about an hour and a half they'd finally finished bagging up the dope.....

"Let's count it up to see how much we bagged up," Double J said.

"We gone twelve blows in a pack, whoever sell the pack get twenty dollars, and turn us in a hundred," Slim said. "How much we gone pay people to run the joint," Double J asked? "We ain't worried about that right now we gone run the joint ourselves. Once it pick up then we'll put people in play to run the joint. We'll worry about what we gone pay them when that time come," Slim said.....

As they sat at the table counting up the dope Slim begin to wonder who was they gone get to work the packs.....

"Shiiit who we gone get to work the joint," Slim asked? "My lil cousins gone work the joint. They been sweating me for the last couple days about when we gone open up the joint, so they can work. They juvenilles, so if they catch a case they momma's can just sign them out from the police station," Double J said.....

Once they finished counting the dope up it came out to twenty packs, and seven odds. They bagged up $2,070 not including the two blows in each pack for the pack workers to get paid.....

Slim begin doing the mathematics in his head.....

"So if we got two stacks off ten grams then we gone get atleast twenty stacks off of the whole hundred grams," Slim said. "Shiit we gone get more than that if the dope is a bomb, and it can take more than three pills a gram," Double J said. "Yep showl is," Slim said.

"Go grab the tape outta the closet," Slim said.....

When he came back with the tape Slim examined it.....

"Yeah joe this tape perfect," Slim said.....

They put twelve bags on a strip of tape, then put another strip of tape over the bags.

They put the tape over the bags in order for the dope to stay fresh, and so none of the workers wouldn't dip in the bags.....

Double J and Slim grabbed the dope and a .45 automatic and went to pick up Double J's cousins, and set up shop in Argale Park.....

They posted up and the corners and in the park.

One of Double J's cousin walked through the hood telling all the dope fiends that they were passing out free dope in Argale Park. They dopefiends rushed to the park and spreaded the word.....

The two niggas that stood in the park, Double J's cousin was the ones passing out the samples to the dopefiends.....

A couple hours later the park was filled with dopefiends shopping for dope.

Double J and Slim couldn't believe how fast, and how many dopefiends were coming to buy dope.

Judging by the large amount of dopefiends that were coming to buy dope, so soon, Double J and Slim knew they had some good dope.

"Damn lord look how many dopefiends waiting in line to shop," Slim said. "That's cuz the dopefiends that we gave samples to went and told everybody that we got good dope, word of mouth travel," Double J said.

Within two days and one night Double J and Slim sold the whole hundred grams.....

"Lord who we gone buy some more dope from," Slim asked? "That's a good question," Double J said.

As they continue to smoke and ride through the hood they remained silent trying to figure out who they'd start buying weight on the dope from.

"We gone have to start buying from Phill," Double J said. "Phill got good dope but it aint a bomb," Slim said. "How you know, you don't even use dope," Double J said. "I can tell from the numbers his dope spots put up. His spots put up a little numbers but they aint all that," Slim said. "Who else we gone buy dope from, we gone have to get it from Phill," Double J said.....

"Ride through Lexington and see if he out there," Slim said.....

As they made it on Lexington they seen Phill standing on the corner with a gang of niggas standing around him on his security.....

"A Phill check it out Lord," Slim said.....

Phill walked towards them smiling.....

"Where's my money at," Phill said. "What money," Slim asked? "My g, what else money. I heard ya'll been tipping outta the park," Phill said. "We'll get the money we owe you a little later on," Slim said. "It aint even been a whole week," Double J said. "So what I want my money, ya'll been tipping," Phill said. "Aigh't we got you," Double J said.

"How much you'll sell us twenty five grams of dope for," Slim asked? "Three thousand," Phill said. "That's kinda high aint it," Double J said. "Naw that's low, anybody else I charge one fifty a gram. I'm only charging ya'll like one twenty five a gram, at one twenty five a gram twenty five grams suppose to come out to thirty one twenty five, but I just said a even three stacks, I aint tripping over a hundred and twenty five dollars. Look right I got shit I gotta do, is ya'll gone need that twenty five grams or not," Phill asked? "Yeah we need it now," Double J said. "I can't get it for ya'll right now but I'll have somebody get it for ya'll later," Phill said.

"We gone have the g we owe you to when you sell us the twenty five grams, so we'll bring the whole four thousand with us," Slim said.

"I gotta go, I'll holla at ya'll later on," Phill said. "Make sure we get them twenty five grams today our joint is outta work," Slim said. "I got ya'll don't worry about it," Phill said. "A'ight we'll holla at you," Slim said.....

Later on that day they were sitting in Double J's crib chilling, when they got a call from Phill telling them that he was going to send his guy John over with the twenty five grams, and that they needed to make sure the four stacks was counted up right before they gave it to John.....

Once John delivered the twenty five grams they went straight to Doubles J's kitchen table and started bagging up.....

"How many pills we gone use," Double J asked? "We gone use three first to see how the dopefiends like it with three on it," Slim said.....

Both of them begin opening up the seventy five capsules and dumping the inside of the dorms on the table on top of the twenty five grams.....

"Lord if this dope is any good we finna be getting money like never before. Fuck spending our money we need to stack our shit, and get into some real estate, then we can leave the dope game alone," Slim said. "Yeah I agree with you on that. You know all these other niggas be spending their shit, then when it comes time for bound money they can't even bound out for ten or fifteen stacks," Double J said.....

As they continued mixing up the dope they both imagined of riches.....

They next day the put the dope on their joint, and to their surprise the dope fiends loved it.....

They finished that twenty five grams in one day, and was right back at Phill buying fifty grams this time. Phill was a player that liked so niggas doing good get money so he sold them fifty grams for fifty five hundred.....

Once they put that fifty grams out their they thought it would slow down some because the dopefiends would know from the last twenty five grams that they aint selling the same dope they had originally when they first opened up.....

Double J and Slim sat back at the end of the park admiring the veiw of the customers swarming to buy dope. It was as if everytime the pack worker would bring out a new pack the dopefiends would swarm on him like flies to shit.....

"How the hell is our joint tipping like this with Phill's dope, and his joint aint putting up numbers like ours," Double J asked? "That cuz Phill, and alot of these other niggas be putting that crazy shit on they dope, that's why I told you we aint gone use nothing but dorms. Phill nam still checking a bag but their turnover rate is slower," Slim said.....

Within a month Double J, and Slim was the men. Their joint was putting up numbers. They had bought new Cadillacs, new sports cars and all. Their team of workers constantly grew. Ho's coming from everywhere trying to get with them..... Throughout it all they continued to buy dope from Phill.....

Chapter 3

One hot sunny day Double J was simply bending blocks in the hood listening to Al Green puffing on joints that wasn't laced with cocaine when he seen her from the back in those jeans.....

Damn this ho thick as hell, Double J thought to himself.

He pulled up to her; once he seen her face he became disappointed. Aw this Cynthia dopefiend ass, he thought to himself.

Cynthia immediately opened the passenger side door and just jumped in his car.....

"Take me to your spot to get some dope," she said. "I got a few bags in my pocket," Double J said. "What are you doing riding around with dope in your pocket," Cynthia asked? "What else am I doing with dope in my pocket," Double J said sarcastically. "I didn't know you shoot dope," Cynthia said. "Tell somebody, and I'll kill you," Double J said.

They drove to a quiet block on the outskirts of the hood, pulled over and parked.

Double J gave Cynthia the dope to hook it up and put in the needle.

Once she hooked the dope up and put it in the needle she tried handing the needle to Double J.

"Naw you go ahead, ladies first," Double J said.....

With her right hand she shot dope into the veins of her left arm as her eyes rolled in the back of her head, as her entire body felt as if it was taken to a whole nother planet.

Afterwards she passed the needle to Double J.

With his right hand he shot dope into the veins of his left arm.

As Barry White song I'm never gone leave your love played on the radio Double J felt as if he was soaring above the clouds.....

Afterwards Double J dropped Cynthia off at home and went and met Slim at his crib to shake up some dope.....

"I bought a hundred grams instead of fifty," Slim said. "That's cool," Double J said.

"Start busting the dorms down I gotta go use the bathroom, my stomach fucked up from smoking all them lace joints," Slim said.....

Slim came out the bathroom and seen Double J sitting at the table nodding and scratching.

"Damn nigga you look like you done had a dope," Slim said. "Naw man I'm just sleepy," Double J said.

So they both begin busting the dorms down.

Double J kept scratching and nodding at the table.

This nigga fucking around with dope, Slim thought to himself.

"Lord tell the truth aint you getting high," Slim asked? "Nigga you know damn well I been getting high ever since you've known me," Double J said. "Nigga you know what I'm talking about is you fucking with dope," Slim said.....

Double J paused for a little while.....

"Yeah I fuck around with the dope a little," Double J said. "What made you turn into a dopefiend," Double J asked? "I use to be seeing how dopefiends look after they get high. Some of them looked like it's the best feeling in the world. Some of them be looking like they're walking on the clouds or some shit. Then I start to see how the dopefiends do whatever it takes to get money for dope, that made me want to try some even more, cuz I knew it had to be some good shit. Once I tried it, it felt like heaven on Earth. No lie, am a be a dopefiend forever. Am a get high til I die," Double J said.

Slim looked at Double J with a smirk on his face thinking to himself, this nigga done lost his mind.....

"Niggas always trying to belittle dopefiends, when they get high they motherfucking self off all type of shit. A drug addict is a drug addict. It don't matter if you smoke weed, lace weed, tut cocaine, tut dope, or shoot dope you still a drug addict," Double J said. "I can agree with you on that cuz I smoke more lace joints than some people use dope," Slim said.

"We gone have to start paying somebody to bag up this dope this shit a headache," Slim said. "Straight up," Double J said.....

Days to follow Slim begin to admire how suave Double J was as he was high off dope.

As he walked, talked, drove, ate, smoke cigarettes, and each and every way he maneuvered was super cool when he was drunk off dope.....

Before long Slim begin asking Double J a gang of questions on how it feels to be high off dope.....

"You steady asking me about how it feels to be high off dope. My best answer is you wont know how it feels until you try it," Double J said. "I'm scared of needles," Slim said. "You aint gotta shot it, you can tut it. But it aint nothing look shooting it, as that dope run up your veins, it's the best high you'll ever experience," Double J said.

133

Slim was still hesitant to try dope he let his pride get in the way, he knew certain people looked down on dopefiends.....

A couple days later at a club with these two lesbian chicks he dated and paid for sex he begin wanting to try some dope again.

The lesbian chicks Tricey, and Reese did it all, besides dope. They snorted lines of cocaine, smoked lace joints, regular weed, and smoked leaf.....

After downing a few drinks at the club. The girls sat at the table snorting line after line of cocaine, secretly not in the publics eye.

"Damn ya'll gone fuck around and O.D.," Slim said. "That's only if you use dope, you ain't gonna find to many people O.Deing of cocaine, although you can O.D. off cocaine," Reese said.

"Have ya'll ever fucked around with dope before," Slim asked? "Hell naw, we aint no motherfucking dopefiends," Tricey said. "Shiiit ya'll get high off every thing else," Slim said. "Everything besides dope," Tricey said.

"I heard that dope is the best high known to mankind," Slim said. "Yeah me to. But it takes control over your body, you gotta have it or your body wont be able to function right. And I heard the sickness is a motherfucker," Tricey said.

"I wanna snort a line or two to see how it feels," Slim said. "So you wanna be a dopefiend," Reese said sarcastically. "Naw I just wanna snort just one bag of dope to see how it feels. I want ya'll to snort it with me," Slim said. "Hell naw," Reese said. "Let's all three of us try it together," Slim said.....

For almost an hour at the club Slim tried convincing the girls to snort a bag of dope with him, and it worked.....

Slim pulled up to his dope spot.....

"Tyrone who working Lord," Slim asked? "Ush working," Tyrone said. "Why don't I see nobody shopping," Slim asked? "It's kinda slow right now, but you can best believe it'll be a gang of customers in line in no time," Tyrone said.

"Go get me three bags of dope, and hurry up Lord," Slim said.

Tyrone rushed to go get three bags from Ush, and brought it right back to the car..... Slim took the dope and smashed off.

Slim parked a few blocks over from his joint.....

He tore open a bag of dope with his teeth and laid it on one of the girls cigarette box. He tore a piece of the paper off his match box. He scooped up half the dope and snorted it like a pro.

He sat the Newport box on the dash and leaned back in his seat to feel the total effect of the dope.

Within seconds Slim had his door opened bent over throwing up his guts.

I'f that shit gone have me throwing up like that I don't even want none, Tricey thought to herself.

After Slim finished throwing up he snorted the other half of the dope off of the Newport box.

He laid back in his seat and relaxed for minutes and begun to feel the effect of being drunk off dope.

The girls then snorted their bags.

As they laid there high they all thought within their own silent minds that dope was the best drug known to men.....

Slim, and both women winded up in a motel room. Slim dick stayed on hard all the while. Slim had heard of the dope dick, but didn't know that it was this intense.....

For the entire week to follow Slim snorted dope, and smoked laced joints each day.

One morning as Slim went home he got into it with his main girlfriend. She was tired of him spending nights out, and cheating on her..... She through some hot coffee on him, and swung on him a few times leaving him with a few minor scars on his face..... Slim stormed out the house and went to his joint.....

Slim pulled on the joint got two bags of dope pulled around the corner to blow them.....

He pulled back around to his joint sat on the hood of his car smoking a lace joint, thinking of all the good times, and the bad times he had, had with his girlfriend..... He was still a little pissed off cuz she put her hands on him.....

Double J pulled of laughing.....

"So I see you having problems with you girl," Double J said. "How you know," Slim asked? "Cuz I see you sitting there faced all scratched up looking crazy, I know you aint let no nigga do it to you, because we'll be in war right now," Double J said.....

Slim tossed the duck of the joint on the ground, and bailed in with Double J, and Double J pulled off.....

"Man this ho crazy as soon as I walked through the door she get throwing shit, hollering, srceaming, and swinging," Slim said. "We all go through problems with women, that's been going on since the beginning of time," Double J said.....

"Pull over for a minute I need to take care of some business," Slim said.

Double J pulled over and put the car in park.

"What you gotta piss or something," Double J asked? "Naw I need to take care of something else," Slim said.

Slim pulled out his pack of cigarettes. Then pulled out a bag of dope, opened it with his teeth and poured it on the cigarette box..... Double J remained silent couldn't believe what he was seeing.

Slim then pulled out a small piece of a straw and snorted the entire bag of dope. Double J just sat there looking at him like he was crazy.

Slim fired up a cigarette, and looked at Double J and asked, "Is my nose clean." "Yes it's clean," Double J said.

"I can't believe you sat there and snorted a bag of dope after you been getting down on me after you found out I was getting high," Double J said. "I been seeing how good you been looking when you high off dope, it be like you be walking on clouds or some shit, and I wanted that feeling so I tried it, and I love it," Slim said. "I told you it was a bomb, especially if you shoot it," Double J said.....

Double J begin smiling and pulled off listening to Barry White's song Ecstasy, as they drove to the mall.....

Once they made it inside the mall Slim became so happy with seeing all the ho's there that he had forgot all about what him and his girl had went through earlier.....

Slim winded up getting a gang of numbers from ho's.

As they entiered this one shoe store Slim couldn't take his eyes of this white chick. She was raw as hell. She was about 5.6", 140 Ibs., a red hed, with black eyeline around her red lipstick, with hazel blue eyes. She looked like a model or some shit.

Slim decided to walk over and strike up a conversation with her.....

Slim came to find out that her name was Angie, she lived on the north side of town. Twenty years of age with no boyfriend, no kids, or none of that. They exchanged numbers, and went their seperate ways.....

All the rest of the day Slim couldn't stop thinking of Angie she just looked so good to him.....

Slim went home that night, and made up with his girl, as they got down within break up to make up sex.....

Slim had never been with a white woman before but always wanted one..... The next day Slim winded up giving Angie a call, he thought she was gone be on some phony shit, but he was wrong she was real cool.....

Slim and Angie starting hanging out together damn near everyday..... One of the things Slim liked about Angie was that she genuinely liked him for him; she wasn't like the other woman that he'd fucked around with, the was only interested money one way or the other, Angie wasn't.....

Within a couple months Slim left his main girl for Angie, and moved in with her.....

Within several months Double J and Slim found there dope habits increasing. Having to spend more money to support their habits.....